WHAT
HAPPENED
TO US?

WHAT HAPPENED TO US?

GR8 RELATIONSHIPS

EQUIP PRESS

Colorado Springs

WHAT HAPPENED TO US?

Published by Equip Press, Colorado Springs, CO

First Edition: 2022
What Happened To Us? / GR8 Relationships)
Paperback ISBN: : 978-1-958585-12-2
eBook ISBN: 978-1-958585-13-9

EQUIP PRESS
Colorado Springs

CONTENTS

WHAT HAPPENED TO US?

"I thought when I got married life would be simple and easy."

"I expected married life to be like walking through a field of sunflowers on a beautiful cool day."

"My wife was different when we were dating, and I thought she wouldn't change. Now all she does is nag me about the kids."

"He just comes home and sits and watches sports. What happened to the man who used to hug me and talk to me about his dreams?"

Do we truly understand relationships and marriage the way God designed them? Or do we bring unrealistic expectations into our relationships? Do we think we can change the other person? What is God's design for relationships? Consider the following scenario and see if any of it resonates with you.

Life is Not a Bed of Roses

Joan and Ed have been married for 15 years. They have two kids, ages 10 and 8. When Joan and Ed married they agreed that Joan would stay home and manage the household so that Ed could focus on his work and provide for her and the family. At first Joan thought this was a great idea, because it allowed her to retire from her teaching job, which had become stressful for her in the last few years. Ed always provided her plenty of money to manage their household budget, save for emergencies and retirement, and to manage their home the way she wanted to. This allowed her to do work at their church and volunteer in the community.

When their first child (Justin) was born he did not sleep through the night until he was about six months old. Ed, a sound sleeper, never got up to help with Justin. One night when she was particularly tired, she woke Ed up and asked him to give Justin a bottle and rock him back to sleep. Drowsy, Ed said he had a big presentation in the morning and needed to get his rest. He convinced her that he would help the next time.

About that time, as a busy consultant, Ed's travel schedule started to pick up and he was out of town at least eight nights each month. Joan expected him to give her a break when he got off the road, on the nights he was home, but he was mostly exhausted after several days on the road working with tough clients. This continued for a couple of years until Catherine, their second child, was born.

Fortunately, Ed's job duties changed so he was no longer on the road, but as a team leader at his consulting firm he seemed to stay at the office later than he used to. He always made it home in time for dinner and now helped put the kids to bed some nights, but typically crashed in front of the TV watching whatever sports were in season.

Through the years Joan confided in Cindy (her neighbor) that she was a little discouraged about her life with Ed. One Monday morning, Joan reached out to Cindy to see if they could have a chat. They decided to meet for coffee at Cindy's house after they had dropped off their kids at school.

When Joan arrived, Cindy opened the door and gave Joan a big warm smile. Joan was surprised at herself as tears welled up in her eyes. Cindy responded with a big hug.

She released Joan and gently held her arms, softly looking her right in the eyes and asked, "What's up, friend?"

Joan just shook her head and continued to weep quietly.

Cindy comforted her friend and said, "Let's go have some coffee and crumpets. I have the ones you like so much."

On the way to the kitchen, Cindy grabbed a couple of tissues from the tissue box on the side table and gave them to her friend.

Joan silently nodded her head and they went into the kitchen. Cindy told Joan to sit at the kitchen table while she fixes their coffee and crumpets and brought them to the table.

By now Joan has relaxed, so Cindy continued to show caring for her friend. "So, what's got you upset?"

Joan answered candidly, "My relationship with Ed is just not what I always dreamed of and hoped for. I imagined walking hand-in-hand with my husband through a beautiful field of flowers and that life would be fun and adventuresome. I dreamed we would take trips together and maybe even work in a volunteer ministry sometimes. It just feels like he works all the time, spends little time helping me with the kids. I know I should be appreciative because I don't have to work outside the home, but I have a tough job! I often feel aggravated that he doesn't help with the household chores, or even the kids. Most days he comes home upset from work and just sits in front of the TV watching whatever sports are in season."

Cindy asked, "Have you talked to him about it?"

"Several times, but it seems we just get into a fight, then I apologize, and nothing changes," Joan explained.

"Have you thought of talking to a marriage counselor?"

"Of course, but he won't even talk to me about it, I doubt he would agree to pay money to talk to someone else about our problems," Joan said.

"Maybe you should just explain that you love him, and you want what's best for the family, and just ask him if he will. I know he cares about you, he just may be unaware of how unhappy you are."

Cindy prayed for Joan and her marriage. Then they finished up their coffee and treats and said their good-byes.

What Happened to Joan and Ed?

You may relate to this story based on what is going on in your marriage. Primarily, Joan and Ed have a breakdown in relationship expectations that isn't being addressed. Perhaps this has to do with their understanding for God's divine design for relationships. God is very clear about how He created Man and Woman in His image and how He created the roles for Men and Women based on how He designed them. Let's explore God's design for relationships, starting with the fact that He made Man and Woman in His own image.

Relationships Based on God's Image

The basis for relationships between men and women is founded in the fact that we were made in God's image. As the scripture below points out, He created male and female in His own image.

> *Then God said, "Let Us make man in Our image, according to Our likeness; let them have dominion over the fish of the sea, over the birds*

of the air, and over the cattle, over all the earth and over every creeping thing that creeps on the earth." So God created man in His own image; in the image of God He created him; male and female He created them. Then God blessed them, and God said to them, "Be fruitful and multiply; fill the earth and subdue it; have dominion over the fish of the sea, over the birds of the air, and over every living thing that moves on the earth."

Genesis 1:26-28, NKJV

This first and foundational passage in scripture articulates the functional aspect of the creation of man. The first part of the statement of purpose notes that man is made in the image and likeness of God (1:26a). That purpose is reiterated with the added nuance of gender distinction (27). The scripture does not describe what man is like, rather what he is to be and do. Just as images or statues represented deities and kings in the ancient Near East, so man, as the image of God, was created to represent God Himself as the sovereign over all creation.

This bold metaphor is spelled out beyond question in Genesis 1:26b, which explains what it means for man to be the image of God.

Then God said, "Let us make mankind in our image, in our likeness, so that they may rule over

*the fish in the sea and the birds in the sky, over
the livestock and all the wild animals, and over
all the creatures that move along the ground."*

Genesis 1:26, NIV

After God blesses Adam and Eve, He gives them a
mandate in verse 28.

*God blessed them and said to them, "Be fruitful
and increase in number; fill the earth and subdue
it. Rule over the fish in the sea and the birds in
the sky and over every living creature that moves
on the ground."*

Genesis 1:28, NIV

The key words in this statement of purpose are
the verbs "rule" (1:26, 28) and "subdue" (v. 28). Hence
man is created to reign in a manner that demonstrates
God's lordship and domination (by force if necessary)
over all creation. Now if that is true, the creation of
man and woman is part of the theological center of
the Bible. This means the creation of man and woman
needs to be understood in its entirety, so that we have
clarity about how and what they were created for. But
first, consider what theologian Dr. Roy Zuck[1] said. He
states that man is created in the image of God to do
the following:

- Represent God Himself as the sovereign over all creation.
- Reign in a manner that demonstrates his lordship, his domination, by force if necessary, over all creation.

The second phrase will be tough to accept by those who worship creation more than the Creator. Anyone who has an unhealthy focus on environmental elements believe that man is the problem for the earth. Without taking that trail, consider that man is not only to show his lordship, his domination, but also to rule as a representative of God Himself. Which, of course, implies stewardship.

So, God put man here to rule, reign and have dominion, but that was changed when Eve and Adam chose to follow Satan's plan not God's. Satan's deception of Eve and the ultimate disobedience by both Adam and Eve put the earth under the rule of Satan. He is now the ruler of this world. He is the one with dominion, as you can see in these verses:

> *Now is the judgment of this world; now the ruler of this world will be cast out.*

John 12:31, NKJV

. . . of judgment, because the ruler of this world is judged.

John 16:11, NKJV

Since man's sin somehow put Satan in charge as ruler, God's plan of salvation will ultimately reestablish mankind as the ruler. So, consider salvation this way: it is deliverance from one place or state to another. This means salvation takes mankind from its current status back to the original plan.

Therefore, while salvation is an awesome gift by our gracious Father, it is not the central theme of God's Word. Man's creation to be ruler of this world is the central theme, and salvation is the amazing instrument God uses to revoke Satan's rule and hand it back to mankind.

This underscores the importance of Genesis. Unfortunately, it is too easy to see the first few chapters in Genesis as only the story of beginnings. It is vastly more important, especially for relationships and marriage. In fact, the first three chapters of Genesis tell us about the following (and more):

- Man's creation and design (what he was designed to do).
- Woman's creation and design (what she was designed to do).
- The foundation used for both of those designs.

- The importance of and how designs are used in marriage.
- The contract for Godly marriage.
- The blueprint for how we sin.
- The structure we follow as the path of least resistance to sin.
- Problems for marriages when we are not following God's roles.
- Woman's Judgment (Curse) and its impact on relationships and life.
- Man's Judgment (Curse) and its impact on relationships and life.

Genesis is critical to understanding the entirety of God's revelation. It provides the *how* and *why*.

Comparable Helper

In His supreme design, God knew that it was not good for man to be alone, so He decided,

. . . I will make him a helper comparable to him.

Genesis 3:18, NKJV

Notice that his *helper* is comparable to him. One is not better or more valuable than the other, God's relationship design started right there in the Garden, where He established creation with built-in and *comparable* roles. Then, God actually created Eve from Adam's rib. Thus Adam proclaimed,

> *"This is now bone of my bones*
> *And flesh of my flesh;*
> *She shall be called Woman,*
> *Because she was taken out of Man."*

Genesis 3:23, NKJV

Further, man and woman are meant to live in relationship outside of their original family with their parents, cleave together and become one flesh. They were designed and created to be in relationship in order to accomplish God's purposes in the earth.

> *Therefore a man shall leave his father and mother*
> *and be joined to his wife, and they shall become*
> *one flesh.*

Genesis 3:24, NKJV

As you can see, the creation story drives everything about the design of human beings, and specifically men and women. Good relationships require depending on and trusting in God, because He designed us and knows what will work best for us.

REFLECTIVE QUESTIONS

- How does God's image play into the creation of man and woman?

  _____

  _____

  _____

  _____

  _____

- Looking at what happened when Adam and Eve believed the serpent and disobeyed God, how does this relate to your personal relationship with God?

  _____

  _____

  _____

  _____

  _____

- What is the importance of the "helper" being comparable?

  _____

  _____

_____

_____

_____

- How does the notion of the "helper" being comparable play into your personal relationship with your spouse or significant other?

_____

_____

_____

_____

_____

- How would you use "comparable helper" in a dialogue about alternative lifestyles and same-sex marriages?

_____

_____

_____

_____

_____

THE IMAGE OF GOD IN RELATIONSHIPS

Genesis provides the *how* and *why* foundation for understanding the design for men and women. God's whole purpose throughout the Bible is to bring mankind back into the purpose of God's original design, which is to rule and reign over the earth with Him. God created man and woman in complimentary relationships and gave them specific purposes and roles that relate to who He is.

Man's Design and Purpose

Looking at Genesis chapter 2, God provides insight into the design of men and women. The following verses indicate the specific reasons God created man.

> *. . . before any plant of the field was in the earth*
> *and before any herb of the field had grown.*
> *For the* Lord *God had not caused it to rain*
> *on the earth, and there was no man to till the*

> *ground; but a mist went up from the earth*
> *and watered the whole face of the ground. And*
> *the* Lord *God formed man of the dust of the*
> *ground and breathed into his nostrils the breath*
> *of life; and man became a living being. Then*
> *the Lord God took-the man and put him in the*
> *garden of Eden to tend and keep it.*

Genesis 2:5-7, 15, NJKV

In these verses we see that there was no man to *till* the ground or *work* the ground. God put man in the Garden to *tend* and *keep* it. In the Hebrew *tend* means to labor, work, serve and till. The word *keep* is translated *to have charge of, protect or preserve.* So it is clear that man is designed for work and activity. This doesn't mean that every man is literally working in farming or gardening, so there is a broader implication. The first verb in verse 15, is translated as *tend, work, dress or cultivate.* In Hebrew this definition implies, *labor, work, serve, till* and sometimes means *enslavement.*

Here's what Webster's Dictionary says:

- Tend: to be in charge of, manage, operate, to take care of.
- Work: physical or mental effort directed toward doing or making something.
- Dress: to till and cultivate land, apply fertilizer, prune, and trim.

- Cultivate: till, prepare land for growth; plant, tend, harvest, or improve by labor and skill.

The second verb in the verse, *keep,* is translated keep, or take care of. In Hebrew the definition is *have charge of, protect, preserve, watch, guard or restrain.* Webster's Dictionary definitions are:

- Keep – to protect, guard, or defend; to have, take charge or care of, to look after, maintain for use.
- Take care – careful or serious attention, protective or supervisory control, to provide physical needs, help, or comfort.

Guarding and protecting obviously require labor, effort, or work, but they also have a relational element to them. This is why God decided that man needed a helper. Please note that God said man's aloneness was not good; man didn't say that.

And the Lord God said, "It is not good that man should be alone; I will make him a helper comparable to him." Out of the ground the Lord God formed every beast of the field and every bird of the air, and brought them to Adam to see what he would call them. And whatever Adam called each living creature, that was its name. So

Adam gave names to all cattle, to the birds of the air, and to every beast of the field. But for Adam there was not found a helper comparable to him.

Genesis 2:18-20, NKJV

Notice that God did not speak about Adam's feelings or opinion in this situation. God saw Adam's need, just like God sees our needs and knows them before we do. Adam was probably like many men today who are blissfully ignorant of the fact that they need a helper. Unfortunately when men treat their wives improperly and don't value their role they are in a sense saying to God, "I despise your gift."

Finally, God's design of man included oneness with woman.

Therefore a man shall leave his father and mother and be joined to his wife, and they shall become one flesh.

Genesis 2:24, NKJV

Man's need for companionship clearly shows that the combination of man and woman's design is good. When you learn about the foundation of man and woman's design, you will see that their designs complement each other. Man's design works best when a woman is included, and vice versa.

Woman's Design and Purpose

And the Lord God said, "It is not good that man should be alone; I will make him a helper comparable to him."

Genesis 2:18, NKJV

God designed woman because man needed a helper who was comparable to him. He actually created her out of Adam's flesh. Many people think that the role and value of *helper* is less than the one who needs the help. That is what Satan wants people to believe: if women do not have the same role as men, they must not have the same value. That is the same lie he tells everyone, everywhere: If you do not have a large or prestigious role, it means you are less valuable as a person.

If you understand the *way* God uses the word helper it can be humbling and amazing for both men and women. The Hebrew word used in *ezer,* and it occurs in the Bible 21 times. It means help, support, aid and designates assistance, or more often assistant. God actually describes Himself as a helper through the psalmist. Look at Psalm 121.

I will lift up my eyes to the hills—
From whence comes my help?

My help comes from the Lord,
Who made heaven and earth.

Psalm 121:1-2, NKJV

So being designated as a helper puts you in good company! Being a helper is a high calling and what women are made for. In essence the helper looks at life through God's eyes and acts like God because her role elevates service over self. Again, she is not less-than, just in a different role.

Woman is also made in God's image. She is designed for relationships and helping, which is not demeaning or derogatory. Her design indicates her need for belonging and relationships. She tends to need safety and security as well.

God is the perfect creator. He knows precisely how things and people fit together best, and He created woman as the perfect companion for man.

To summarize the complementary purpose of men and women, let's look at their roles. Men are designed to work to provide, protect and preserve, and women are designed to help, nurture and support. The two roles perfectly complement each other, just as God planned it.

REFLECTIVE QUESTIONS

For Men

- Looking at your own life, what are you doing to actually *tend* and *keep* in your marriage and family?

_____

_____

_____

_____

_____

- What can you appreciate about your wife or significant other as your comparable helper? What can you notice about how and why you need her?

_____

_____

_____

_____

_____

_____

- How will you communicate that to her?

_____

_____

_____

_____

_____

_____

For Women

- Reflect on what it means to be a helper in the same way that the Holy Spirit, part of the three-in-one Godhead, is a helper. List everything that is important about that role.

_____

_____

_____

_____

_____

_____

- How do you view your role as being a helper to your husband or significant other? If you feel perturbed by that, stop and reflect on the root cause of your frustration. If it is the result of the way you have been treated, write down specific examples, then pray over what you have written and ask God to show you how to share it with the other person if appropriate.

_____

_____

_____

_____

_____

_____

- Make a list of what you appreciate about your husband or significant other in terms of providing, protecting and preserving.

_____

_____

_____

_____

_____

_____

OUR RELATIONSHIPS WITH GOD

Your relationship with God is reflected in your relationships on earth. God is not a policeman in the sky waiting for you to make a mistake so He can pummel you. Your Father in Heaven constantly pursues your best and cares for you, so much that He became human and paid the price for you to be with Him in Heaven. He came down to earth, suffered brutal beatings and wounds to take your place for sin. He did this because He desires that you live with Him eternally in Heaven, yet it's more than that. He wants a beautiful relationship with you that human experience cannot adequately describe. It is close and intimate, but not confining; peaceful and content, yet challenging; connected, yet somehow unique.

Think about a person who you love very deeply. You might notice that you love the look of their hair, or certain little endearing habits they have. Whether it is a spouse or a child, you value them and want them around you, just because. You have a deep abiding love for them and you know so much about them that other people do not know. So it is with God. He knows everything about you. Jesus told his disciples in the book of Matthew that even though He takes care of the sparrows you are worth more than they are. Imagine it, He has numbered every single hair on your head.

> *Are not two sparrows sold for a penny? Yet not one of them will fall to the ground outside your Father's care. And even the very hairs of your head are all numbered. So don't be afraid; you are worth more than many sparrows.*

Matthew 30:29-31, NIV

Do you know what this means? It means that the God of the universe wants a relationship with you! He would love nothing more than you sitting at His feet, asking Him questions, listening to His teaching, enjoying His presence, and feeling His divine care for you. Yet you may be scurrying around trying to *do* something for God and miss the point. Consider the story of Martha and Mary. Jesus was visiting their home, and Martha was running around cooking and serving, trying to make everything just right. She was frustrated with Mary sitting at Jesus' feet, drinking in every word. She even *scolded* Jesus for Mary's behavior.

What did our Lord say? He suggested Martha was focusing on the wrong activities.

*Now it happened as they went that He entered
a certain village; and a certain woman
named Martha welcomed Him into her
house. And she had a sister called Mary, who
also sat at Jesus' feet and heard His word. But
Martha was distracted with much serving, and
she approached Him and said, "Lord, do You
not care that my sister has left me to serve alone?
Therefore tell her to help me."*

*And Jesus answered and said to her, "Martha,
Martha, you are worried and troubled about
many things. But one thing is needed, and Mary
has chosen that good part, which will not be
taken away from her."*

Luke 10:38-42, NKJV

Focusing on God, His Word, and building a deep
relationship with Him may seem foreign to you. The
church doesn't always do a great job of teaching people
how to enjoy a deep and fulfilling relationship with
God. On top of that you have a distractor, who hopes
to deceive you and encourage you to doubt God's good
intent toward you. Satan whispers and questions, "Is
God *really* all that good? Are you *sure* he is not holding
something back from you?"

A perfect example occurred in the Garden when the
serpent convinced Eve to try the beautiful fruit of the

tree of knowledge of good and evil. Essentially, this was the only thing God said *not* to do. He had placed Adam and Eve in a perfect environment with everything they needed. Essentially the serpent was attempting to interfere with the relationship mankind (Adam and Eve) had with God. He challenged their faith in God by suggesting God was *holding out* on them. Only one thing would separate them from God's fellowship and intimacy.

> *And the* LORD *God commanded the man, saying,*
> *"Of every tree of the garden you may freely eat;*
> *but of the tree of the knowledge of good and evil*
> *you shall not eat, for in the day that you eat of it*
> *you shall surely die."*

Genesis 2:16-17, NKJV

Only one thing could re-establish that intimate relationship with God.

> *For by grace you have been saved through faith,*
> *and that not of yourselves; it is the gift of God,*
> *not of works, lest anyone should boast.*

Ephesians 2:8-9, NKJV

> *And without faith it is impossible to please God*
> *. . .*

Hebrews 11:6, NKJV

Without faith in God's eternal provision of Jesus' death, burial, and resurrection you face the penalty of sin passed to you from Adam and Eve. You face consequences much worse than the judgments. You face damnation and eternal separation from God. When you belong to Christ, you are an heir to His promises.

> *And if you are Christ's, then you are Abraham's seed, and heirs according to the promise.*

Galatians 3:19, NKJV

Believers, without faith in God's daily provision of Jesus' life in them, do not have deliverance from the power of sin. They do not have peace and joy, and face the consequences of sin, which includes the loss of a walk with God.

One *big* difference for you is the number of temptations and opportunities to break your relationship with your heavenly Father. Adam and Eve had *one thing*; you have many things. However, if you are a child of God, you have the life of Christ and the Holy Spirit in you to provide the energy to stay in relationship with God, which Adam and Eve did not have.

It's interesting how the serpent questioned the fact that if Eve ate of the fruit she would die. Eating the forbidden fruit severed the intimacy with God, because it was in direct disobedience to Him. Satan's whole purpose is to steal, kill and destroy. He's crafty

about that, encouraging us to go against God and
doubt Him.

> *The thief does not come except to steal, and*
> *to kill, and to destroy. I have come that they*
> *may have life, and that they may have it more*
> *abundantly.*

John 10:10, NKJV

Relationships with God and Others

You can compare this intimate relationship God
wants us to have with Him to strong relationships
between husband and wife. Think about the elements
we have discussed so far. We talked about God's intimate
caring for us, since He has the hairs on our head
numbered. Think about attentiveness to your spouse.
What if you spent as long as it took to count every hair
on your spouse's head? That would be pretty attentive,
wouldn't it? Or what if you took the time to actually
tell your spouse every day why you love her. Imagine
how that would impact your relationship. Imagine what
would happen if you reminded your husband what you
appreciate about him every day?

Think about the Martha and Mary story. Martha
was running around *doing*, while Mary attentively drank
in every precious word from the Lord Jesus.

Martha even said to Jesus, essentially, "I'm running around here doing all the work, why don't you get Mary to help me."

What if couples stopped running around, *doing, doing, doing,* and actually sat down and listened to each other, drinking in every word the other person had to say? How might that impact your relationship with your spouse?

Let's look at the notion of faith.

We as Christians can have faith that God will always provide for us. He always has our best interests at heart, even when we might not like what is going on. By faith, we believe that our sins are washed away. By faith we believe that Jesus dying on that tree at Calvary was a replacement for the punishment we deserve, and more importantly, it's a way to restore that intimate relationship He planned between you and Him. When you trust Him, your relationship deepens.

When we say to God, "I trust you, even though I don't understand what's going on right now. I'm going to trust You and be obedient to You," that goes a lot farther to create a stronger relationship than complaining.

"God, I want some answers! I don't like what's going on, and you haven't made my life exactly like I planned or wanted."

Consider this same response to God when you might be communicating with your spouse. This goes either way.

As a wife, you can say to your husband, "Why did you decide to be a pastor instead of a lawyer? Now we can't send the kids to summer camp." That's extreme, but the notion is it says to the husband, "I don't trust you to make the right decisions."

What if the husband says to his wife, "Dinner is not ready, hot and steaming when I get home from work, so I don't trust you to manage the household." That would not go very far in developing the relationship.

Even worse, those statements are truth serum about your relationship with God! Relationships, especially close ones, are your practical theology displayed in real-time. That is why the Apostle Paul told us,

> . . . *work out your own salvation with fear and trembling* . . .

Philippians 2:12, NKJV

This passage does not mean working *for* your salvation, it says working *out*, which means every minute you either display Jesus or your sin nature. So, when you show trust in God it can show up as trust in your spouse. Instead of jumping right to judgment about their decision, you trust God and either go with their decision or have a healthy conversation about it.

Notice that this is not based on the trustworthiness of your spouse, it is based solely on your trust in God, which implies an intimate relationship with Him.

Without that relationship, your sin nature jumps directly to judge them in comparison to your *perfect* ways.

With God, by not questioning why something has happened in a certain way, you show trust in Him. When you love your heavenly father, you trust that He has your best in mind. In marriage, when you think about how much you love your spouse, you trust him or her. Even if you don't agree with everything they think or say, love supersedes any doubts you have, which allows you to trust them and show faith in their decisions. When you start with love you are not judgmental. When you love someone, you pursue their best.

Let's consider the statements listed earlier.

The wife who says, "Why did you decide to be a pastor instead of a lawyer? Now we can't send the kids to summer camp." If she pursues his best, she focuses on what's best for him and trusts that God will provide through her husband. This is love because she is focused on what's best for her husband. Rather than focusing on what she wanted, what if she said, "I know you have made the best decision for our family. You have always supported us and I trust you, and have faith in what you have decided."

Also, a spouse showing faith in her husband demonstrates faith in God, since ultimately, the Lord is our provider. Look at what Abraham said when the Lord provided a sacrifice other than Abraham's son Isaac.

*Then Abraham lifted his eyes and looked, and
there behind him was a ram caught in a thicket
by its horns. So Abraham went and took the ram,
and offered it up for a burnt offering instead of
his son. And Abraham called the name of the
place, The-Lord-Will-Provide; as it is said to
this day, "In the Mount of the Lord it shall be
provided."*

Genesis 22:13-14, NKJV

Let's look at the husband saying to his wife, "Dinner
is not ready, hot and steaming when I get home from
work, so I don't trust you to manage the household."
What if he pursues her best by trusting that dinner isn't
ready because she *was* managing the household. Rather
than jumping to judgment because of what he wants,
because he loves her, he believes the best and pursues
her best when his sin nature assumptions try to get him
to believe differently.

Any time you love you have the capacity to trust
them and have faith in them, even when facts show
otherwise. How is that possible? Because you love God,
which means you obey Him, which in turn means you
love others because He said that is the best way to live,
especially in marriage and family. You can look at them
through God's love and God's eyes, which leaves no
room for judging them.

Judgments Impact Marriages

Understanding the real problems that the judgments create for men and women simplifies the problems in relationships and marriages that seemed so complex before.

When you grasp the underlying foundation of the image of God, His designs and judgments, relationships between men and women will stop looking like some of Albert Einstein's abstract math equations. And, understanding the links between the judgments, designs, and self-absorption, you gain new insight into your behavior and those things that help and hurt marriages.

For example, this graphic represents what the judgments do to marriages. It is simple enough that you can look at it and have some basic understanding of what it is saying without knowing about designs and judgments. If you know the foundation of the chart you become someone that can help a couple through a difficult time.

Most people could look at the chart and say it makes sense but would consider it only one of hundreds, maybe thousands of things that could happen. Knowing what you currently know from God's Word, this is a "root cause" for marriage problems and failure.

When you add typical comments to the chart it adds to the reality, and in some cases, to the pain that a person is feeling from the relationship. A woman might say things like:

- "You spend so much time at work and so little time with me and the kids."
- "Your golf is more important to you than your family."
- "Why can't we have some time for just us?"

And the statements from the husband might sound like this:

- "There is so much going on at work. I have so much to do."
- "I wish I could just have some time to myself to relax and do something other than work."

The wife wants the relationship with the husband to fulfill her and the husband wants his work to fulfill him. The woman's basic need from her design is security and that is not being met. The man's basic need from his design is significance and that is not being met. The judgments set up relationships, and marriages in particular, to struggle and fail.

But God has the answer!

Remove Judgments and Impact

God has the answers for your marriage and relationships to succeed. God's methods are always the best. He is the only One that can resolve the pain and struggles that come from the judgments that He established.

Relationships work when men and women do what God asks. When a husband loves his wife the way that Christ loves the church, and a wife respects her husband as God asks her to, the impact of judgments against each other is gone. A husband truly loves his wife as much as Christ loves the church and a wife submits to her husband as she submits to the Lord. Ultimately, the relationship each of them has with the Lord impacts their relationship with each other.

> *Husbands, love your wives, just as Christ also loved the church and gave Himself for her,*

Ephesians 5: 25, NKJV

> *Wives, submit to your own husbands, as to the Lord.*

Ephesians 5:22, NKJV

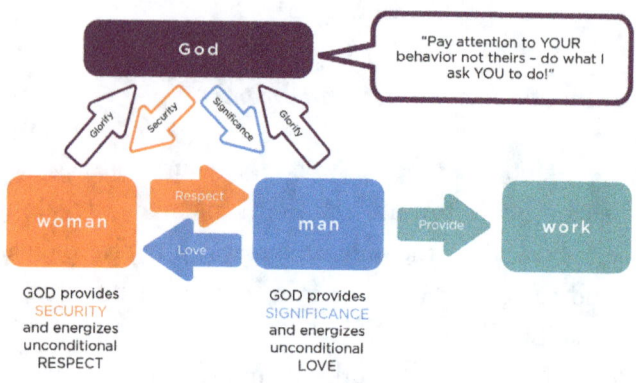

A woman who starts respecting will stop controlling. A man who starts loving (pursuing his wife's best) will stop ruling her, stop abdicating leadership and perform excellent work, because it is another way to glorify God.

Please notice the imaginary statement from God in the graph above.

"Pay attention to *your* behavior, not theirs – do what I ask *you* to do!"

The judgments get you to focus on how your needs are not being met and encourage a focus on getting other people or things to meet those needs. God's statements allow each of us to choose, and are not intended to make others choose. Yes, you are to speak God's truth into another person's life, but it is God's job to change them.

The power to overcome the judgments comes from God. But, even though God can, He does not force us to choose His way. That is your responsibility.

He states that a wife is to respect her own husband (Ephesians 5:22) and that a husband is to love his wife as Christ loves the church (Ephesians 5:25-31).

Please notice what God *does not* say, "Husbands get your wife to respect you. And, "Wives, make sure that your husband loves you."

When you start focusing on what God asks of *you*, you *stop* participating in your judgment. The judgment focuses your attention on what the other person is doing or not doing. *Start* paying attention to *your* behavior, not your spouse's behavior. Consider what the gospel of Matthew says.

> *And why do you look at the speck in your*
> *brother's eye, but do not consider the plank*
> *in your own eye? Or how can you say to your*
> *brother, 'Let me remove the speck from your eye';*
> *and look, a plank is in your own eye?*

Matthew 7:3-4, NKJV

REFLECTIVE QUESTIONS

- Make a list of things you can do or say to show your spouse how precious they are to you.

_____

_____

_____

_____

- Are you sitting at God's feet listening to Him during your Bible reading or quiet time? If your prayer time sounds like you giving God a litany of what to do, stop and ask Him to reveal His heart to you. What does He say?

_____

_____

_____

_____

- Think about this. "The purpose of prayer is to realign your mind to depend on and relate to my Perfect Father God, not get answers." If that is true, how would that change your prayer life?

_____

_____

_____

_____

_____

- How can you apply quiet and intimate time with God to spending time with your spouse, just listening and appreciating them?

_____

_____

_____

_____

_____

_____

- How does Satan distract you from your deep relationship with God? For the next two weeks, make a note every time you hear Satan whispering something intended to make you doubt God's goodness and good intentions for you.

_____

_____

_____

_____

_____

- What can you do to grow a stronger faith in God, and deepen your relationship with Him?

  _____

  _____

  _____

  _____

- How can you apply trusting and having faith in God to trusting and having faith in your spouse? How will you express that?

  _____

  _____

  _____

  _____

- How is judgment impacting your relationship with your spouse? Make a note during the next week, every time you see yourself judging your spouse's shortcomings. Ask God to forgive you and show you how to change your attitude.

  _____

  _____

  _____

  _____

  _____

- Husbands, write down ways you can show your wife that you love her as Christ loves the Church.

_____

_____

_____

_____

_____

- Wives, write down ways you can show your husband that you respect him.

_____

_____

_____

_____

_____

- Meditate on the scriptures below in your quiet time each day. Make a note of what God reveals to you.

_____

_____

_____

_____

_____

Husbands, love your wives, just as Christ also loved the church and gave Himself for her,

Ephesians 5:25, NKJV

Wives, submit to your own husbands, as to the Lord.

Ephesians 5:22, NKJV

GOD'S DESIGNS FOR MEN AND WOMEN

Men's Design

Consider a farming metaphor: man is designed to provide, protect, and preserve the seed. He is designed to work, cultivate, keep, take care of, manage, and develop what is planted. And all this is done best in companionship with woman, because his design needs compatible help, suitable companionship in the process. That companionship element with woman is encouraged when God states that man is to separate from mother and father and be joined as one with a woman.

Why is the design of man so important to know? Because not knowing or paying attention to the design of something increases the probability of misuse. Consider a time you decided to use a butter knife as a screwdriver. You can make it work, but that is not what it was designed to do. Knowing your design is critical, otherwise, you do not know if you are using it properly.

Men, you are designed for work and activity. Three words that adequately describe a man's design are: Provide, Protect and Preserve. Using these words is an easy way to remember the design of man.

Women's Design

Going back to the farming metaphor, women are designed to help, nurture, and support the seed. A woman bears, births, assists, aids, and gives relief to what was planted. Like man, a woman does not do this alone, because she is the complementary companion to help man and his aloneness, which is often unrecognized by man. Finally, a woman's design is best utilized in combination with man's design, joining in complementary oneness.

Women, you are designed with an emphasis and strength to employ all the many facts required to *relate*. Whatever your endeavor, whether leading or following, when you use your innate ability to relate, you focus on your strength.

I ask every woman leader who I coach, to consider leading with their relational design instead of trying to be powerful. Sometimes corporate structures encourage women to act incongruously with their God-given design. Many accomplished women leaders carry that natural relational design to its highest and best use.

Overall, the words Help, Nurture and Support describe a woman's design.

Design of Woman Saves Her

Looking at the above description of woman's design brings clarity to 1 Timothy 2, specifically verses 8 through 15.

> *1 Therefore I exhort first of all that supplications, prayers, intercessions, and giving of thanks be made for all men, 2 for kings and all who are in authority, that we may lead a quiet and peaceable life in all godliness and reverence. 3 For this is good and acceptable in the sight of God our Savior, 4 who desires all men to be saved and to come to the knowledge of the truth. 5 For there is one God and one Mediator between God and men, the Man Christ Jesus, 6 who gave Himself a ransom for all, to be testified in due time, 7 for which I was appointed a preacher and an apostle—I am speaking the truth in Christ and not lying—a teacher of the Gentiles in faith and truth.*
>
> *8 I desire therefore that the men pray everywhere, lifting up holy hands, without wrath and doubting; 9 in like manner also, that the women adorn themselves in modest apparel, with propriety and moderation, not with braided hair or gold or pearls or costly clothing, 10 but, which*

is proper for women professing godliness, with
good works. 11 Let a woman learn in silence
with all submission. 12 And I do not permit
a woman to teach or to have authority over a
man, but to be in silence. 13 For Adam was
formed first, then Eve. 14 And Adam was not
deceived, but the woman being deceived, fell into
transgression. 15 Nevertheless she will be saved in
childbearing if they continue in faith, love, and
holiness, with self-control.

1 Timothy 2:1-15, NKJV

The creation of man and woman as well as the sin in the Garden of Eden in Genesis chapters 1-3 provide the proper context for the above scripture. Without those important contextual elements, you will be speculating about what God is telling you in 1 Timothy 2.

Men are designed to work while women are designed to relate. Then in Genesis, Adam and Eve sin by eating from the tree of the knowledge of good and evil. Finally, God judges both of them for sinning; Eve in 3:16 and Adam in 3:17-19.

Here are the three critical elements from Genesis 3:

Element One

Sin occurred in the context of a marriage that did not follow God's designs and roles. Adam followed instead of leading or protecting Eve. And Eve led instead of following and supporting Adam. How can you know the roles were not followed? Read Genesis 3:17, the first part of the judgment on man.

> *Then to Adam He said, "Because you have heeded the voice of your wife, and have eaten from the tree of which I commanded you, saying, 'You shall not eat of it"* . . .

Adam was judged for listening to or obeying Eve, not God. Providing, Protecting, and Preserving can only happen when we follow God's instructions. When you trust God, you will escape "the corruption that is in this world through lust" (as stated in 2 Peter 1:4). When you trust someone or something other than God, bad things happen!

Element Two

Woman's relational design was judged in 3:16, making her relationships with her children and husband painful and less fulfilling. (We will say more about this in a future book.)

Element Three

Man's work design was judged in 3:17-19 making his ability to work painful and less fulfilling. (We will say more about this in a future book.) And, for the immediate context of 1 Timothy, everything after chapter 1 is about church organization and conduct. Chapter 2, verses 2 and 3, set the tone for what follows:

> "...lead a quiet and peaceful life in godliness and reverence. For this is good and acceptable in the sight of God our Savior..."

In 1 Timothy, from the beginning of chapter 2 to the end of chapter 6, the recurring theme of order and roles is presented. God is a God of order and tells us how life will work best – following the order and roles He provides in His Word for society, church, and family. There are numerous places in God's Word speaking about order, and here in 1 Timothy the roles in church and family help maintain order.

In 1 Timothy 2 you can summarize verses 9-14 with the "order and role" theme. Starting in verse 9 "in like manner" picks back up on the theme of order referring back to the "...quiet and peaceable life with all Godliness and reverence..." stated in verse 2. Notice the theme in the following verses:

- Verses 9 and 10 – Women's outward appearance is to have an order. (In the Greek *adorn* is about order.)
- Verse 11 – Women's learning is to have an order.

- Verse 12 – Women's and men's roles are to follow an order…
- Verse 13 – …because roles and order were established in the beginning.
- Verse 14 – When the order was not followed, bad things happened.

Since all of the previous verses were about order and roles, verse 15 is most likely carrying the same theme. Without knowing the context is about order, designs, roles, and original sin, verse 15 does not seem to fit.

Finally, before you put it all together, consider two words in verse 15, *childbearing* and *saved*. First, the word "saved" is not referencing eternal salvation, which can only come through faith in Jesus Christ. The context of the passage is to believers, so it cannot be about eternal salvation, meaning hell to heaven. The way "saved" is used in God's Word is always critical. You will become confused about eternal salvation when you miss the many times saved refers to temporal salvation.

For example, even though "saved" is not used in 2 Peter 1:4, the temporal salvation idea is well stated. You will "…escape the corruption that is in this world through lust." Additionally, you will be "saved" when you follow the steps outlined in 2 Peter 1:5-9. That is great news! Your eternal salvation also provides temporal salvation as you follow God's Word. In other words, you are saved for eternity by faith in Jesus Christ's death, burial and resurrection and you can be saved daily, escaping the corruption in this world, by choosing to follow God's desires, instructions, and invitations to a better life.

Second, childbearing is not only about the birthing process, but by implication it involves all of the maternal role and more broadly, the role and design of a woman. The broadest implication can be drawn simply from the realization that "childbearing" can only be used for a woman and not for a man. So, I see childbearing as best understood as a reference to the unique role and design of a woman.

Therefore, combining the meanings above, the phrase "saved in childbearing" would make sense when stated as: ***A woman will be delivered; she will escape corruption in this world, as she operates in her role and design.***

Why is this message needed? It is similar to what God states in 1 Corinthians 11. God tells women how to remove the impact of the judgments He put in place back in Genesis 3:16-19. Ever wonder why there is a structure of competition and conflict between men and women? It is a result of the judgments that were a consequence of sin. Do not miss what Satan does with the judgments. The more he gets the world to focus women on equality, being more like a man, the more the judgments create conflict and strife in marriage as well as between men and women.

The design of anything specifically makes it unique for a specified purpose. Design seldom works well if it is considered interchangeable. But the world, and many churches, promote men and women as interchangeable parts. God's Word states otherwise. God designed women to fulfill a high calling, a calling of a Helper like God is to us. When that design is ignored, bad things happen – the corruption of the world through lust becomes a destructive force in our, and in this context, her life. When a woman ignores her design and role, focuses on equality to a man, she asks her judgment to reign supreme in her life and bad things happen.

God's Word initiates and promotes the equal value of women, and God promotes the design and role differences, and the judgments are still in effect. All three are true!

That is why the second part of the verse follows with the conditional *if*. Just like eternal salvation is conditional upon faith in Jesus Christ, a woman's temporal salvation, and beating the judgment and corruption in this world, is dependent on three elements; faith, love, and holiness – all of which are a woman's choice.

Therefore, a woman continuing to live in her design to help, nurture, and support is extremely counter-cultural. That means she will choose the following:

- Faith – she chooses to trust that God's order, role and design are best for her. Her "who said so" becomes God, nothing else.
- Love – she chooses to use her design and role for the benefit of others, not herself. She chooses helping, nurturing, and supporting instead of self-absorption.
- Holiness – she chooses to be set apart, unique, different from the world rather than conformed to it.
- Self-control – she chooses to allow the Holy Spirit to control-self. Remember that self-control is not something you create, the power of the Holy Spirit creates it in you.

To paraphrase verse 15,

A woman will be delivered from her judgment and the corruption in this world as she operates in her design if she continually chooses:

- to trust that God's order, role and design is best for her.
- to pursue the best for others using her role and design.
- to set herself apart from the world's view of women by using her role and design as God desires.

This only happens by choice and self-governance, allowing the power of the Holy Spirit to control her flesh or sin nature which rebels against God's order and design for life.

A woman will be delivered from her judgment and the corruption in the world as she continually chooses to operate in her God-given design.

Women, your design by God is wonderful, completely unique from man, and when used as God designed, saves you from your judgment and the corruption in the world.

It is your choice. And what a benefit you receive when you choose God's way.

REFLECTIVE QUESTIONS

Men

- Based on the farming metaphor, man is designed to provide, protect, and preserve the seed. He is designed to work, cultivate, keep, take care of, manage, and develop what is planted. Describe how you are operating in God's design for you in your life.

_____

_____

_____

_____

_____

- Describe some ways where you can re-establish God's order into your marriage, work relationships and your home.

_____

_____

_____

_____

Women

- Based on the farming metaphor, women are designed to help, nurture, and support the seed. A woman bears, births, assists, aids, and gives relief to what was planted. Describe how you are operating in God's design for you in your life.

_____

_____

_____

_____

_____

- As a woman leader, how can you apply your relational design to successfully fulfill your purpose and calling in life?

_____

_____

_____

_____

_____

_____

- Watch for situations where you have led your husband rather than supported? Notice whether there is a habit that needs to be changed.

Examine why you have gotten into that habit if
that is the case.

_____

_____

_____

_____

_____

- What are your thoughts about the "Design of a
  Woman Saves Her?"

_____

_____

_____

_____

_____

THE ROLES HE CREATED WORK TOGETHER

God created men to work that He could fulfill his role to provide, protect and preserve. This is what God our heavenly Father does for us too. So, the man is acting in the earth as God does. He is representing God's image in his assigned role.

Women, designed as helpers who help, nurture, and support are also created in God's image. He wants relationship with each of us and longs to help and support us in life's journey. In fact, the Holy Spirit, part of the trinity, is actually referred to as the helper. Look at what Jesus said.

> *Nevertheless I tell you the truth. It is to your advantage that I go away; for if I do not go away, the Helper will not come to you; but if I depart, I will send Him to you.*

John 16:7, NKJV

His disciples were concerned about what they would do without Him, but He assured them the *Helper* would come to support and help them in anything they needed to accomplish. In fact the Helper would empower them to do their work.

The roles of provide, protect, and preserve (for a man) and help, nurture, and support (for a woman) in God's plan do not indicate that anyone is less than another or that their role is less important. This has to do with God's order as indicated in 1 Corinthians.

> *But I want you to know that the head of every man is Christ, the head of woman is man, and the head of Christ is God.*

1 Corinthians 11:3, NKJV

God's order and authority are not about one person ruling over another. If you think about a man leading a woman in a relationship in the context of their design and God-given roles, you can see that this brings order. Think about a leader in the military on a battleground. Someone has to be the leader and others follow the leader or you would have chaos. The infantry submitting to their commander saves lives and empowers the troops to win the battle. Having a leader and a follower makes sense to accomplish their mission. In the same way, a husband leading his wife moves them together in a direction to accomplish what God has for them. If they are not operating on the same team, they cannot stand. Even though Jesus was talking to the Pharisees about their accusation of Him, in Matthew 12, this also applies to a modern-day household.

> . . . *Every kingdom divided against itself will be ruined, and every city or household divided against itself will not stand.*

Matthew 12:25, NIV

Leading with God's Authority

Someone needs to be in charge, but a key for success in this is thinking about the fact that leaders with God's authority serve others. God asks leaders to use His authority correctly by freeing people and being gentle. Doing those two things will result in leading correctly.

As a reminder, leadership is misunderstood. Much of the time, all of the attention is focused on the leader. A self-absorbed view of leadership is misguided, yet many people gravitate to that. That creates an ineffective leadership structure. If people aren't doing what you want you become defensive and let them know you are the boss, the big man, the leader. When you try to prove you are the leader, most often you are no longer leading. You act like a dictator and worse, you react and respond to situations rather than lead.

Leadership is not about you! Leadership is about serving others. Servant Leaders follow God's leadership, doing what He says is right and best. They understand God's truth on which the stand and think about their relationship with God first. Servant Leaders value followers enough to spend time and energy developing them. These leaders are not dependent on trying to please followers or others, nor do they consider followers in second place. They encourage followers in self-governance empowering them to employ their giftings and abilities to the mission at hand.

Leaders Don't "Have to" Lead

If you "should, must, have to" lead, you will create a big problem for yourself and the people you lead. At minimum, you will decrease your energy to lead, because you are doing it from obligation, not desire.

If you lead, because you "have to," then you will probably have a bad attitude and expect others to show their appreciation for what you do. Satan wants you to have that attitude, because he knows you are focused on yourself, not others. You can choose whether to lead in the way that God directs.

The great military General Norman Schwarzkopf eloquently summed up service above self in the quote below:

"The Army, with its emphasis on rank and medals and efficiency reports, is the easiest institution in the world in which to get consumed with ambition. Some officers spend all their time currying favor and worrying about the next promotion — a miserable way to live. But West Point saved me from that by instilling the ideal of service above self — to do my duty for my country even if it brought no gain at all. It gave me far more than a military career — it gave me a calling."[2]

Paul's Leadership Style

The apostle Paul provides another great example of leadership the way God intended it. His style is well-outlined in 2 Corinthians 11. Starting with how deeply he cares for and identifies with the people he leads.

Oh, that you would bear with me in a little folly—and indeed you do bear with me. For I am jealous for you with godly jealousy. For I have betrothed you to one husband, that I may present you as a chaste virgin to Christ.

2 Corinthians 11:1-2, NKJV

He offers protection for and exhorts those he leads in two portions of this book in scripture.

But I fear, lest somehow, as the serpent deceived Eve by his craftiness, so your minds may be corrupted from the [a]simplicity that is in Christ.

For if he who comes preaches another Jesus whom we have not preached, or if you receive a different spirit which you have not received, or a different gospel which you have not accepted—you may well put up with it!

2 Corinthians 11:3-4, NKJV

But what I do, I will also continue to do, that I may cut off the opportunity from those who desire an opportunity to be regarded just as we are in the things of which they boast. For such are false apostles, deceitful workers, transforming themselves into apostles of Christ. And no wonder! For Satan himself transforms himself into an angel of light. Therefore it is no great thing if his ministers also transform themselves into ministers of righteousness, whose end will be according to their works.

2 Corinthians 12-15, NKJV

Paul is unwavering and sober regarding his abilities and position.

For I consider that I am not at all inferior to the most eminent apostles. Even though I am untrained in speech, yet I am not in knowledge.

But we have been thoroughly manifested among you in all things.

2 Corinthians 11:5-6, NKJV

He refused the burden of those he led.

Did I commit sin in humbling myself that you might be exalted, because I preached the gospel of God to you free of charge?

8 I robbed other churches, taking wages from them to minister to you.

9 And when I was present with you, and in need, I was a burden to no one, for what I lacked the brethren who came from Macedonia supplied. And in everything I kept myself from being burdensome to you, and so I will keep myself.

10 As the truth of Christ is in me, no one shall stop me from this boasting in the regions of Achaia.

11 Why? Because I do not love you? God knows!

2 Corinthians 11:7-11, NKJV

Paul defends the ministry (but not himself), pointing out his higher calling as a true minister of the gospel of Christ.

But what I do, I will also continue to do, that I may cut off the opportunity from those who desire an opportunity to be regarded just as we are in the things of which they boast. 13 For such are false apostles, deceitful workers, transforming themselves into apostles of Christ.

2 Corinthians 11:12-13, NKJV

Paul speaks the truth and communicates clearly with those he leads. Men who are leading their spouses and families have an obligation to clearly communicate and speak God's truth.

I say again, let no one think me a fool. If otherwise, at least receive me as a fool, that I also may boast a little.

17 What I speak, I speak not according to the Lord, but as it were, foolishly, in this confidence of boasting.

18 Seeing that many boast according to the flesh, I also will boast.

19 For you put up with fools gladly, since you yourselves are wise!

20 For you put up with it if one brings you into bondage, if one devours you, if one takes from you, if one exalts himself, if one strikes you on the face.

21 To our shame I say that we were too weak for that! But in whatever anyone is bold—I speak foolishly—I am bold also.

2 Corinthians 11:16-21, NKJV

Paul suffered for those he led, just as Jesus did, and husbands do as leaders in their households and relationships.

> *Are they Hebrews? So am I. Are they Israelites? So am I. Are they the seed of Abraham? So am I.*
>
> *23 Are they ministers of Christ?—I speak as a fool—I am more: in labors more abundant, in stripes above measure, in prisons more frequently, in deaths often.*
>
> *24 From the Jews five times I received forty stripes minus one.*
>
> *25 Three times I was beaten with rods; once I was stoned; three times I was shipwrecked; a night and a day I have been in the deep;*
>
> *26 in journeys often, in perils of waters, in perils of robbers, in perils of my own countrymen, in perils of the Gentiles, in perils in the city, in perils in the wilderness, in perils in the sea, in perils among false brethren;*

27 in weariness and toil, in sleeplessness often, in hunger and thirst, in fastings often, in cold and nakedness—

2 Corinthians 11:22-27, NKJV

Paul boasts in God's strength and ability and trusts Him rather than himself. The same way Jesus did; He often said He only did what the Father directed Him to do. The same way a husband in a home leads according to God's strength and his trust in God.

besides the other things, what comes upon me daily: my deep concern for all the churches.

29 Who is weak, and I am not weak? Who is made to stumble, and I do not burn with indignation?

30 If I must boast, I will boast in the things which concern my infirmity.

31 The God and Father of our Lord Jesus Christ, who is blessed forever, knows that I am not lying.

2 Corinthians 11:28-31, NKJV

If you, as a leader in your family and household, find yourself acting like an authoritarian dictator, think about two amazing leaders, Jesus and the Apostle Paul, and emulate their leadership style. You'll find plenty of examples in the scriptures. One thing to always remember in your leadership and relationships is to keep God at the center. Then you will never go wrong.

REFLECTIVE QUESTIONS

- How well do you apply the Apostle Paul's leadership style?

  _____

  _____

  _____

  _____

- Based on the attributes listed below, how can you apply Paul's example to your own life leading your family or leading in a relationship?
  Cares deeply for and identifies with those he led.

  _____

  _____

  _____

  _____

- Offers protection to and exhorts those he led.

  _____

  _____

  _____

  _____

  _____

- Unwavering and sober about abilities & position.

  _____

  _____

  _____

  _____

- Defends position and ministry, but not himself.

  _____

  _____

  _____

  _____

- Refuses to be a burden or dependent on those he led.

  _____

  _____

  _____

  _____

- Speaks the truth, communicates clearly with those he led.

  _____

  _____

  _____

- Suffers for those he led.

_____

_____

_____

_____

- Boasts in and trusts God not himself.

_____

_____

_____

_____

Working Together in the Modern Family

As you read this story, think about what resonates with you in the story. Do you see yourself in these situations? Think about how God's designs and roles are played out in the scenario. What are possible challenges this couple might face in weighing their God-given roles and personal desires and aspirations?

Mary and James and Family

James and Mary are married and have four children. James owns his own business as a construction contractor, so he works long hours and has lots to manage keeping the business going. James typically leaves the home around 7:00 am and does not return home for dinner until 6:00 or 7:00 pm, and is sometimes called away in the evenings to solve an issue with a customer or subcontractor.

Mary is a CPA by training and worked in a large accounting firm right out of college. She and James met at a networking event and became business friends before their attraction to each other led to true love and marriage. The first few years of their marriage both of them worked in an effort to build up as much savings and investments as they could before having children. Mary was not only a brilliant CPA, with a good head for math and business, she was also a skilled and successful department leader for the firm she worked for. She had an uncanny knack for helping teams communicate and perform efficiently. One of the reasons she was such a great leader is that she was always open to mentor new team members and encouraged them to asked lots of questions of her and other team members.

After about five years of marriage, James and Mary decided to start their family. They had candid discussions about how their roles might shift as their family grew. The first child, Drew, was born healthy, weighing in at 9 lbs. After he was born, Mary stayed home from work for six months, then found herself feeling lost in motherhood. She was so accustomed to going to a busy, thriving job every day, that she started to feel unfulfilled and unchallenged mentally. James' business was succeeding and growing by leaps and bounds, so he found it hard to get home and play with Drew before Mary put him down for the night.

James had a growing sense of responsibility to provide for the family, but he also knew his wife was adjusting to her new role as stay-at-home mom. He also felt compelled to protect her sanity. He thought maybe he should hire someone to help her around the house, so she could work part-time or do something outside the home. Or perhaps he could suggest she get a babysitter sometimes and go have dinner with a friend when he had to work late. They discussed those options at dinner one night, but Mary didn't like the idea of hiring a babysitter so she could go out with girlfriends. She told James that working was all or nothing for her. She couldn't see working in her field part-time, but was open to hiring a nanny so she could go back to work full time. After several discussions and looking at the cost for her to work outside the home, they decided she would continue to stay home with Drew.

One night, James was out managing his business until 10:00 pm. He checked in with Mary to let her know what was going on with his client. Mary had had a long day too. Drew, now teething, was fussy all day long. She was pretty frustrated with the situation that day, because she hoped to get a break and get some help with Drew when James came home. She didn't show her frustration on the phone, knowing that James was just doing a good job to provide for the family. She didn't bother fixing dinner because they had some leftovers from the night before and he could always order something in or pick up something on the way home. She just crawled into bed early and was fast asleep when he got home.

A couple of years go by and Mary has continued to stay home with Drew, not working, but managed to keep her mind sharp by staying active with a professional group of CPAs that she knew from her corporate days. She and James had a second child, William. William is all boy, and just as active as Drew. James' business continues to grow, but he hired some competent managers, who freed him from some of the customer and contractor issues that he sometimes had to deal with in the evening. He has made a conscious effort to make it home for dinner every night, even if he had to log on to his laptop after the boys went to bed.

Fast forward five more years. Mary and James now have four children, Drew was 9 and William was 7. They both went to Montessori school and their younger sisters Catherine, who was 4 and Julia, who was 2, go to Mother's Day Out twice a week. Mary was very active at her sons' school as a volunteer and helped the school with fundraising and financial reporting. She really enjoyed herself because she had connected with some other moms who worked in corporate and professional jobs, who had also stayed out of the workforce to raise their families. She made a conscious effort to make sure her kids communicate with each other when they have disagreements. She felt it important that she should not be in the middle of every spat they had with each other.

James and Mary have had their struggles, like any married couple, but have managed to figure out how to work as a great team raising their young family. James felt like everything in his life is perfect. Mary doesn't feel bad about her life, but she's started to notice that she felt disconnected from James. Yes, they went out to nice dinners and even on weekend getaways without the kids sometimes, but she felt like James was more of a business partner than a soulmate and husband. She began to feel that something was really missing in their relationship and in the family. One night, after all the children are fast asleep, they got into a deep discussion.

After Mary finished cleaning the kitchen and straightening up the living room, she sat on the couch beside James, who was reading the paper.

"James, we need to talk."

"Oh?" he said, putting the paper down on the floor. "What's up?"

She looked at him steadily and said, "I just feel like something is missing between us. It seems we are both focused on the kids. It leaves little time for us."

"Well, what can I do about it?" he asked, as if talking to a client. "Do you want me to take you on another trip or hire some help for you at home? I know you have given up a lot by giving up your career."

Mary smiled a half smile, almost chuckling to herself at James' business-like demeanor. "Trips are always nice. I just feel like we have lost touch with each other."

"Wow, I'm shocked to hear you say that. I thought we were going along as a stellar team. I never played on any baseball team my whole life that is as well-run as we and our family are."

"We are great at managing activities, and coordinating schedules, showing up at every event for the kids. But . . ." her voice trailed off.

"But what, just tell me," James said, feeling a little insecure at this point about what she might say next. He didn't say it, but thought to himself, "Me? Disconnected? You should see some of the guys I work with. They could care less about their families."

"I know you are exhausted with all you put into your business, but the kids and I need to connect with you."

"What are you thinking will help?"

Mary spoke carefully, sensing James' irritation. "Nothing major. Maybe we just have better conversations. We both just tell each other stuff. I'm probably guilty too."

"Okay. I'll do whatever you want me to," he said as he looked off, not really looking at anything.

"I don't want you to just do what I tell you. I want you to work it out with me," she explained.

"But I'm not the one who is unhappy about anything in our life. I don't know where to start. I feel like I do everything anyone wants me to do. Honestly, at the end of the business day, I am spent."

Mary understood, "I've been there, I know how intense work can be."

"Mary, I don't think you have 'been there.' When you were working, you didn't have the pressure of five mouths to feed," he said in a frustrated, almost defensive tone.

At this point Mary was a little stunned at what he said and decided not to push any further. "Look, let's continue this another day. I'm going to go take a bath and go to bed."

"Fine by me," he said as he picked up the paper. Then he grabbed her hand and said, "Please don't think I'm blowing this off, I just don't have any ideas right now."

She nodded her head and half smiled, and said, "I understand."

REFLECTIVE QUESTIONS

Thinking about the scenario above, answer the questions.

- How did Mary apply her God-given design to her career as a CPA?

_____

_____

_____

_____

- What do you notice about James using his God-given design in the way he operates in business and with his family?

_____

_____

_____

- What about this story resonated with you? What frustrations in your own life came up while you were reading the story?

_____

_____

_____

- Where do you see opportunities for James to be a servant leader?

_____

_____

_____

_____

What language do you notice from James that indicates he's more work-focused than relationship-oriented?

_____

_____

_____

_____

- What danger signals do you see in this relationship?

_____

_____

_____

_____

STUDY GUIDE

Scripture Meditation

Time: 30 minutes a day

Each day read and meditate on one of the scriptures listed below or as directed by your session leader.
Follow these steps:

1. Get in a quiet place without distraction.
2. Play a praise song, and just listen to the words.
3. Ask God to reveal His heart and meaning to you as you read the scriptures.
4. Write your reflections below or in your journal.
5. Read the scriptures daily so you receive maximum revelation.

Genesis 1:26-28	1 Timothy 2:1-15
Genesis 2:18	2 Corinthians 11:1-2
Genesis 2:24	2 Corinthians 11:3-4
Genesis 2:5-7, 15	2 Corinthians 11:5-6
Genesis 3:24	2 Corinthians 11:7-11
Psalm 121:1-2	2 Corinthians 11:12-13
Luke 10:38-42	2 Corinthians 11:22-27
Ephesians 2:8-9	2 Corinthians 11:28-31
Matthew 7:3-4	Matthew 12:25

1. What is the most significant concept you learned in this book regarding God's design for relationships? How will you apply that?

2. What issues, if any, in your own attitudes did you discover by reading this book?

3. As a leader, what practices will you continue, and how will you change your style based on what you read?

4. What did you learn about God's authority? How will you apply that in your life?

TOOLS

The following tools will enable you to understand yourself and your spouse and how you can work together to handle conflict. The videos listed below are a part of the video course that corresponds to the information in this book. Completing all the courses will be instrumental for you to find FREEDOM!

You can find all these tools (and many more) on our website www.GR8relate.com at the TOOLS tab.

Kolbe Assessment https://gr8relate.com/kolbe

You can trust the validity and accuracy of the Kolbe instrument to show you your strengths and instincts. The Kolbe also helps you easily see and understand how the strengths and talents of one person may not be considered as strengths by another. This critical information will help you bridge the gap between reality and your expectations of them. Once you complete the assessment, you will receive detailed reports that will help you understand your strengths and talents and how to use your strengths in a complementary way with your spouse, family member, or friend's strengths. By understanding your instincts you can more easily discuss your differences, laugh about them, and develop ways to deal with them.

The *Thomas-Kilman Conflict Mode Instrument* (TKI) https://gr8relate.com/tki

The TKI is the world's best-selling instrument for understanding conflict. It helps you see that conflict can be beneficial and useful, instead of thinking conflict as bad. You will be provided detailed information on effectively using all five conflict modes: competing, collaborating, compromising, avoiding, and accommodating.

The *Fundamental Interpersonal Relations Orientation-Behavior*™ (FIRO-B®). https://gr8relate.com/firob

The FIRO-B helps you understand how you interact at work and personal life. This easy-to-complete-assessment will provide critical insights into how an individual interacts with others. This personality instrument measures how you typically behave with others and how you expect them to act toward you.

Individual Videos

Ten Second Summary of GR8 Relationships – https://vimeo.com/164152149
Am I Making This About Me? – https://vimeo.com/164736178
Two Circles – https://vimeo.com/164736180
What Is the Order? – https://vimeo.com/168487959
God the Model for Freedom – https://vimeo.com/168492029
Step 1 – Face Their Humanity – https://vimeo.com/169007008
Confession Insights – https://vimeo.com/169024281

Go Deeper

This book series is designed to help you start finding Freedom in all your relationships. If you want to dig deeper, we've got more! Go here: https://gr8relate.com/video-courses/ These are our FREE courses. You will learn more about your relationships. And if you like what you see, please help us Pay It Forward to help others gain Freedom in their Relationships.

Forms

The following forms will be useful tools as your work through your relationships. You can copy these as you need them. You can also find these and other useful tools at www.gr8relate.com. Click on the Tools tab.

Six Guidelines When Confessing

Right Attitude

- Always think of them as more important than you – (Philippians 2:3-4)
- Have NO expectations about changing them
- Go with a heart that knows you wronged them and will confess your wrong, no strings attached
- Be Humble & Defenseless
- Believe Resolution is Possible
- Slow Your Emotions Down!

> **Philippians 2:3-4**: Let nothing be done through selfish ambition or conceit, but in lowliness of mind let each esteem others better than himself. Let each of you look out not only for your own interests, but also for the interests of others.

Right Words

- When confessing be careful of the words you use
- If you have not confessed to God, you will not like using the words that must be used here
- A Pattern for Right Words.

> ***A Pattern for Right Words***
> ➢ AGREE: I was wrong when I (describe attitude and actions)
> ➢ ACKNOWLEDGE: I realize that this has hurt you (and others)
> ➢ ADMIT: I regret my actions and repent before God and you
> ➢ ANNOUNCE: I plan to (state actions) to help me not do that again
> ➢ Thank you for listening. If there are other items that need to be cleared up, I am willing to discuss those also, now or later.

Right Method

- A personal visit is probably the best overall
- A phone call can be very helpful for tough issues
- A letter is least preferred

Right Time

- Is the time convenient for the other person?
- Is it a time when you would not likely be interrupted?
- What is a danger when thinking of the right time?

Right Communication Style

- Deal gently even if they are not gentle with you
- Slow the emotions down!
- Prepare before and even role-play gentleness
- Use speech seasoned with grace
- Take 100% Responsibility to Communicate
  - Communication is cursed
  - Communication is delicate
  - Understand first, then disagree
  - Don't assume you will be understood
  - Look at them during conversation
  - Speak the "Truth in Love" (Eph. 4:15)

> **Galatians 6:1** Brethren, if a man is overtaken in any trespass, you who are spiritual restore such a one in a spirit of gentleness, considering yourself lest you also be tempted.
>
> **James 3:17** But the wisdom that is from above is first pure, then peaceable, gentle, willing to yield, full of mercy and good fruits, without partiality and without hypocrisy.
>
> **Colossians 4:6** Let your speech always be with grace, seasoned with salt, that you may know how you ought to answer each one.
>
> **Proverbs 15:1** A soft answer turns away wrath, But a harsh word stirs up anger.
>
> **Proverbs 6:16-19** These six things the Lord hates, Yes, seven are an abomination to Him: A proud look, a lying tongue, hands that shed innocent blood, a heart that devises wicked plans, feet that are swift in running to evil, a false witness who speaks lies, and one who sows discord among brethren.

Right Meeting Guidelines

- Create handout (see Meeting Guidelines) for the parties that will be participating
- Ask permission of the other party to send the guidelines to them
- In some situations, select a trusted, wise third party to facilitate
- Use the guidelines even if no third party present
- Look up all the verses in the Meeting Guidelines prior to meeting to refresh your mind to truth

51 Relationship Principles

1. Think of others as important, in fact, more important than you.

2. 3 Simple Guidelines; 3 Simple Questions
   a. Do what is right. Will I do what is right?
   b. Be trustworthy. Will I commit to doing my best?
   c. Do to others as you would have them do to you. Will I pursue the good of and serve others more than myself?

3. Freedom in relationships does not mean license; it primarily involves being a real person and letting others be themselves.

4. Freedom blossoms relationships: control and manipulation limit them.

5. Freedom in marriage allows each person to operate in their design.

6. If people are not free to be themselves around you, then, most likely, your relationships are all about YOU.

7. When freedom and choice are not in a relationship, someone is being controlled (dominated or manipulated).

8. When you cannot be yourself in a relationship, the relationship will become intolerable.

9. When freedom and choice are in a relationship, the whole person (good & bad) is accepted.

10. When you are tense, angry, frustrated, or irritated, it often means someone is not doing the job you assigned them.

11. Your happiness is a lousy job to assign to anyone or anything. Why let someone else control you that way?

12. When you take things personally, you are not operating in freedom.

13. Without freedom in a relationship, someone will be a fake, hypocrite, or liar.

14. If a relationship must satisfy you, you are walking down the manipulation trail (You are saying NO to the relationship and making the relationship about you; freedom is limited).

15. Relationships happen in reality, in real-time, with real people.

16. No one owes you anything in a relationship.

17. The closer you are to change, the greater will be the resistance.

18. To the degree we deny our issues, we will find a scapegoat on which to dump them.

19. Victims are focused on getting their circumstances and those around them to change, not on changing themselves.

20. Victims must be rescued; they are dependent on circumstances or others' changes to make them happy.

21. Draw a line in the sand and create a new past.

22. Give people more than they expect cheerfully.

242 Spring Park Drive, Ste A   Midland, Texas 79705   Phone: 432-682-6823   https://gr8relate.com   Email: info.gr8relate@gr8grp.com

Pursuing Their BEST
— In Work, In Life, In Love

Conflict RESOLVED BluePrint

Remember 4+3+2 Essentials

4 Critical Principles	3 Cardinal Rules	2 Skills	5 Styles
·RELATIONSHIPS: WE, not just ME **·FUTURE**: The Past is OVER **·FREEDOM**: Don't try to change them **KINDNESS**: Kindness instead of winning	**·SLOW** the emotions down **·TALK** until a solution is found ·Seek **TWO**-sided solutions	·Listening ·Asking Questions	·Accommodating ·Avoiding ·Collaborating ·Competing ·Compromising

Evaluate the Conflict: Questions...

Conflict	You	Them	Meeting
·What is it about? ·What are the components? ·How will it impact the relationship? ·Will we 1) battle until the other changes? 2) disagree and end relationship, 3) disagree and keep relationship 4) resolve and keep relationship 5) resolve and end the relationship	·What was my role, contribution? ·What resolution do I want? ·What are my needs, goals? ·Do I need them? ·Are my expectations reasonable? ·What misperceptions might they have of me?	·Am I defining them by their negative behavior? ·What are their needs? ·Do I understand their side? ·What misperceptions might I have of them? ·What buttons do they have?	·What Method? ·What Time? ·What Location?

Set the Ground Rules

3 Cardinal Rules	General Rules		Good Values
·SLOW the emotions down **·TALK** until solution is found ·Seek **TWO**-sided solutions	·Be Clear ·"Speak to the center of the room" ·No attacking or blaming ·One person speaks at a time	·Look at each other when speaking ·All ideas as valid when presented ·Build on each other's ideas ·Explore each idea	·Be Fair ·Be Honest ·Be Responsible ·Be Respectful ·Be Considerate

Open the Conversation

Open and honest about seeking a solution	Partner with them; create a WE atmosphere	Encourage options through shared effort	Narrow the scope – agreement on everything is not required

Listen and Clarify

Focus only on them	Observe what they say	Seek facts with good questions	Summarize; check what you heard	Summarize often	Seek Permission

Value and Seek Options

Criteria for Good Options	Meets one or more shared needs	Meets one or more needs not incompatible with other party	Potential to improve future relationship	Can be supported by all parties
Uncover Options	Seek their options first	Learn from the past	Keep your ears open!	

Establish A Solution

·WE (2-sided solutions) ·Thinking (Slow emotions down) ·Facts (talk)	·Focus on shared needs ·Increase the size of the pie	Behavior specific	Document it

Decide to Follow-up

242 Spring Park Drive, Ste A   Midland, Texas 79705   Phone: 432-682-6823   https://gr8relate.com   Email: support@gr8relate.com

Meeting Guidelines

Be Thankful in Prayer

- Thank God for the conflict – 1 Thessalonians 5:18
- Accept that God has been and is at work in the conflict – Genesis 50:20, Romans 8:28
- Praise God for allowing the sin. Sin is the root problem, not the other person and not God – James 4:1, Romans 6:12-13
- Accept confession and forgiveness are God's answer to conflict
- Ephesians 4:32, Colossians 3:13, 1 Peter 3:8-9

Be Humble

- James 4:6; 1 Peter 5:6-7
- Allow God's grace to permeate your lives – James 4:10
- Recognize both of you are depraved apart from Christ – Romans 3:10-12, Ephesians 2:1-6
- Each of you accepts personal responsibility in the conflict. (Offer no defense. Pride is defensive.)

Be Just & Merciful

- Micah 6:8

Be Gentle

- Deal gently with each other – Galatians 5:22, James 3:17
- Consider the other person as more important than yourself; Philippians 2:3-4
- Do not try to change the other person. (You are responsible for YOU. Pride causes us to focus on their faults.)

Be Gracious

- Use speech seasoned with grace
- Colossians 4:6, Proverbs 15:1, 6:16-19

Be Considerate

- Ephesians 4:15, Proverbs 21:10

Be Renewed

- Christ's life (your new life) and the Holy Spirit's energy are the keys to any resolution
- Galatians 2:20, 5:16, 24-25; 2 Corinthians 5:17

Be Clear

- Speak about the problem, not the person
- Use the "Speak to the Center of the Room" communication style. Pick an object to represent the problem and talk about it, even point at it

Be Honest About Facts & Feelings

Use "I + feel + when" technique

"I + feeling word + when"

1. Begin conversation with a qualifier
   - "I want to tell you how I feel"
   - "I am not asking you to agree with me"
   - Never use BUT after those statements (can be manipulative)
2. State your feelings ("I am really upset")
3. Always use observable behavior
   - "I was hurt when you didn't speak to me last night."
   - NOT, "You always are hurting me"
4. Reframe or "mirror" what is said
   - "What I hear you saying..."
   - "I am not sure that I understand, but let me tell you what I heard."

Love's Current Reality

Score yourself on how you relate to your SPOUSE or a SPECIAL relationship. Use a 1 to 10 scale, where 1 is worst, and 10 is best (10 = Never or Always in the statements below)

1.	I suffer long; I am patient— I always endure evil, injury, and provocation, without being filled with resentment, bitterness, or grudges	
2.	I am kind—I always am gracious toward and do good for others	
3.	I do not envy, I am not jealous—I never compare myself to others, never suspect unfaithfulness, never feel inferior because of comparison	
4.	I do not brag or boast—I never have an "I" problem, never judge or act like I am better than others	
5.	I am not puffed up, proud—I never call attention to myself, never puffed up about myself or my possessions	
6.	I do not behave rudely—I am always courteous, respectful, considerate, chivalrous, gallant	
7.	I do not seek my own—I am never self-seeking or self-absorbed, never have to have it my way	
8.	I am not provoked—I am never easily angered or react to what others are doing to me, always operate on Godly values	
9.	I think no evil—I never keep a list or think of wrongs done to me	
10.	I do not rejoice in evil—I never condone or tolerate evil or wrongdoing and never rejoice when it happens	
11.	I rejoice in truth—I am always delighted to see truth win, delighted when truth is shared with me when I have been wrong, delighted to get constructive criticism	
12.	I bear all things—I always protect others, never share their faults when speaking to others	
13.	I believe all things—I always trust, never suspicious, assuming, or reluctant to believe the best about others	
14.	I hope all things—I always hope for the best without controlling or manipulating	
15.	I endure all things—I always persevere in good and tough times, and I never feel compelled to talk about my problems	

Using the above information, identify 1 or 2 items you would like to enhance. Write an action you could regularly take this month to help you score higher next time.

ENDNOTES

1   Biblical Theology of the Old Testament, Roy Zuck, et al. Moody Publishers, 1991, pps 13, 14.
2   It Doesn't Take a Hero, General H. Norman Schwarzkopf. Bantam Books, 1993.